TAX SALES
FOR ROOKIES

A Beginner's Guide to Understanding Property Tax Sales

STEVE KON

AuthorHouse™
1663 Liberty Drive
Bloomington, IN 47403
www.authorhouse.com
Phone: 833-262-8899

Because of the dynamic nature of the Internet, any web addresses or links contained in this book may have changed since publication and may no longer be valid. The views expressed in this work are solely those of the author and do not necessarily reflect the views of the publisher, and the publisher hereby disclaims any responsibility for them.

Any people depicted in stock imagery provided by Getty Images are models,
and such images are being used for illustrative purposes only.
Certain stock imagery © Getty Images.

This book is printed on acid-free paper.

ISBN: 978-1-6655-2224-3 (sc)
ISBN: 978-1-6655-2223-6 (e)

Library of Congress Control Number: 2021907301

Print information available on the last page.

Published by AuthorHouse 04/29/2021

authorHOUSE

TAX SALES FOR ROOKIES
- COURSE OUTLINE

COURSE DESCRIPTION: TAX SALES FOR ROOKIES

The purpose of this course is to help the novice understand what a tax sale is about, and to guide the investor through a step by step process of acquiring real estate through a tax sale. This guide will address topics such as the difference between tax deeds versus tax certificates. This class also addresses numerous important issues such as the different type of tax sales, researching tax sale properties, preparation for attending the sale, and important legal issues a tax buyer should be knowledgeable on prior to participating in a tax sale.

LEARNING OBJECTIVES: TAX SALES FOR ROOKIES

* Define what a tax sale is

* Understand the pros and cons of the tax sale

* Understand the value of participating in a tax sale

* Understand the differences of tax certificates and tax deeds

* Understand the different types of tax sales

* Learn how to properly research tax sale properties

* Understand the process of how to take a tax certificate and convert it into to a tax deed

TAX SALES
FOR ROOKIES

WHAT IS A TAX SALE?

A tax sale is an opportunity for each county to collect delinquent real estate taxes. All unpaid real estate taxes are auctioned off in the county where the taxes are delinquent.

The laws of a tax sale are governed by state statute. The rules for each sale are controlled by the county in which the delinquent taxes are being sold. Furthermore, the tax buyer must be aware of both county and state laws when participating in a tax sale.

MAIN REASONS TO PURCHASE TAX CERTIFICATES/DEEDS

1. Acquire real estate inexpensively
2. Earn high rate of return on investment

TAX CERTIFICATE VS. TAX DEED

The purchase of a tax certificate is not the same as owning a tax deed. The tax certificate is what the tax buyer receives after buying unpaid taxes. The tax certificate will either be redeemed by the owner, or can eventually ripen into a tax deed for the tax buyer. If the taxes are redeemed by the owner of the property, the tax buyer will receive the interest based on the amount of the percentage he purchased the certificate.

If the owner of the property does not redeem the property, the owner of the certificate can now proceed to acquire the property by following the legal process. After the process has been completed, the tax buyer can now receive a tax deed. The tax deed is the legal document that conveys ownership. The following page shows an illustration of an actual tax deed that was acquired through a scavenger sale held in Cook County Illinois.

TAX DEED-SCAVENGER SALE

STATE OF ILLINOIS)
) SS.
COUNTY OF COOK)

█████████████████████

No. ████████████████ D.

At a **PUBLIC SALE OF REAL ESTATE** for the **NON-PAYMENT OF TAXES** for two or more years, pursuant to Section 21-260 of the Illinois Property Tax Code, as amended, held in the County of Cook on ██ ████████████████, the County Collector sold the real estate identified by permanent real estate index number ___ See Exhibit A ___ and legally described as follows:

See Exhibit A

Section_____, Town_____ N. Range_____ East of the Third Principal Meridian, situated in said Cook County and State of Illinois;

And the real estate not having been redeemed from the sale, and it appearing that the holder of the Certificate of Purchase of said real estate has complied with the laws of the State of Illinois, necessary to entitle him to a Deed of said real estate, as found and ordered by the Circuit Court of Cook County;

I, ██████████████ County Clerk of the County of Cook, ██████████████ ████████████ in consideration of the premises and by virtue of the statutes of the State of Illinois in such cases provided, grant and convey to ___ Stephen Kon ___ _____ residing and having his (her or their) residence and post office address at ___ P.O. Box 241, Joliet, IL ___ _____, his (her or their) heirs and assigns **FOREVER**, the said Real Estate hereinabove described.

The following provision of the Compiled Statutes of the State of Illinois, being 35 ILCS 200/22-85, is recited, pursuant to law:

"Unless the holder of the certificate purchased at any tax sale under this Code takes out the deed in the time provided by law, and records the same within one year from and after the time for redemption expires, the certificate or deed, and the sale on which it is based, shall, after the expiration of the one year period, be absolutely void with no right to reimbursement. If the holder of the certificate is prevented from obtaining a deed by injunction or order of any court, or by the refusal or inability of any court to act upon the application for a tax deed, or by the refusal of the clerk to execute the same deed, the time he or she is so prevented shall be excluded from computation of the one year period."

Given under my hand and seal, this ___████___ day of ___████___ _____ ████

Rev 8/95 ___ _____████_____ County Clerk

4

PROS VS. CONS

PROS

- Purchase property inexpensively
- Earn high rate of return on investment

CONS

- Properties are often in blighted areas
- Need tax deed attorney to guide you through legal process. It is detrimental to make an error in proceeding to tax deed. If an error is made proceeding to tax deed, the consequences could be costly. The results could mean losing your monetary investment and/or losing the right to obtain a deed.
- Need patience in acquiring the deed
- Researching for tax sales is tedious and time consuming

TYPES OF SALES

ANNUAL SALE

The annual sale occurs every year for taxes that have not been paid by the owner.

The bid is based on a percentage rate. In Illinois, the rate earned is anywhere between 0-18%. Bids start at the highest percentage and are bid downward to the lowest bidder.

Annual taxes are redeemed by owner majority of time for the percentage bid on.

Annual taxes purchased must also include any prior years' taxes that have not been paid. They must be paid prior to receiving the tax certificate. Warrant books show any taxes that have not been paid.

A tax buyer can purchase any subsequent taxes without buying them at the tax sale. In Illinois, the tax buyer receives 12% interest if the taxes are redeemed by the owner.

- ✓ Note: After six (6) months, in order for the owner to redeem the property, (s)he must pay <u>double</u> the percentage bid by the certificate holder.

SCAVENGER SALE

The scavenger sale is bid at the auction based on a dollar value, not on a percentage. Bids for all parcels of property start at a base dollar amount and can go to infinity.

The purpose of the scavenger sale is because the taxes were not sold at previous annual sales. The county will not put a parcel in a scavenger sale unless the taxes do not have at least two years of delinquent taxes.

In Illinois, the tax buyer can purchase subsequent taxes and receive 12% interest if redeemed by the owner.

The majority of time the taxes purchased at the scavenger sale will not be redeemed by the owner. There is a high probability of obtaining a tax deed.

✓ Note: Owner must redeem the amount due on taxes, whereas the tax buyer only has to pay the bid amount. The back taxes usually are for amounts considerably more than what the tax buyer has paid.

The following two pages are illustrations of actual tax certificates issued by Cook County in the State of Illinois. The certificate number 03-0010028 is an example of an annual certificate. The certificate numbers 99- 0014492 is an example of a scavenger certificate.

STATE OF ILLINOIS)
) ss
COUNTY OF COOK   )

CERTIFICATE NUMBER ▬▬▬

--CERTIFICATE OF PURCHASE--

FOR GENERAL TAXES AND SPECIAL ASSESSMENTS, A.D. 2003 , ETC.

I, DAVID D. ORR, County Clerk in and for the County and State aforesaid
DO HEREBY CERTIFY THAT ▬▬▬ did, on the day hereinafter set
forth , purchase at Public Auction, at the Court House in CHICAGO, the property designated by
PERMANENT REAL ESTATE NUMBER ▬▬▬ situated in said County for
the taxes, interest and costs due and unpaid thereon for the tax year 2003 and prior and paid
as purchase money on said property the total amount of taxes, interest and costs thereon as
stated herein.

VOLUME ▬▬   PERMANENT INDEX NUMBER ▬▬▬

TAXES	Date of Sale	Rate of Pencent Sold			Total Amt. of TAXES and Interest	Date Paid
	07/21/05	15.00	Tax	218.98		07/21/05
GENERAL 2003			Interest	35.20		
					254.18	
BACK TAX YRS -			Tax Interest			
SPECIAL ASSESSMENT 2004			Tax Interest			
STATUTORY TREASURER FEES			•		212.71	
STATUTORY CLERK FEES					47.00	
PRIOR YEARS' SPECIAL & GENERAL TAXES						
20 2002					141.27	
20						
20						
20						
TOTAL					513.89	
					655.16	

Received this 13 day of **SEPTEMBER** , 2005 , the sum of $ **513.89** the
amount of the purchase money on the above property.   655.16

If the aforesaid property is not redeemed in the manner and within the time provided
by law, the above-named purchaser, his heirs or assigns, will, upon application and compliance
with the provisions of law pertaining thereto, be entitled to receive a deed of conveyance
for said real estate herein described by said permanent index number; provided that unless the
holder of this certificate shall take out said deed, as entitled by law, and file same for
record within one year from and after expiration of the time of redemption, the said certificate
or deed, and the sale upon which it is based, shall from and after the expiration of one year,
be absolutely null.

WITNESS my hand and the official seal at CHICAGO in said County
this 13 day of ▬▬▬ .

Assessee:

Countersigned:

County Treasurer and Ex-Officio Collector
of Cook County

County Clerk of Cook County

STATE OF ILLINOIS)
) SS   CERTIFICATE NO.   ███████████
COUNTY OF C O O K)

CERTIFICATE OF PURCHASE
FOR GENERAL TAXES TWO OR MORE YEARS DELINQUENT, PURSUANT TO SECTIONS 21-145 AND 21-260 OF THE ILLINOIS PROPERTY TAX CODE

I, ████████████ , County Clerk in and for the County and State aforesaid, DO HEREBY CERTIFY THAT   ICON INVES TS INC did, on the day hereinafter set forth, purchase at public auction at the courthouse in Chicago, the property designated by the permanent real estate index number hereinafter set forth, situated in said County, said property being delinquent in the principal sum and for the tax years hereinafter set forth together with statutory penalties, interest and costs thereon, and paid as purchase money on said property the sum hereinafter set forth, such sum being the highest bid for cash received at the auction of such property pursuant to Sections 21-145 and 21-260 of the Illinois Property Tax Code.

VOLUME   423   PERMANENT INDEX NUMBER ███████████

TAX YEARS DELINQUENT ███████████
TOTAL PRINCIPAL AMOUNT DUE   3,088.36   plus statutory
penalties, interest and costs thereon.
DATE OF SALE   ███████ AMOUNT OF SUCCESSFUL BID   250.00

STATUTORY TREASURER FEES   202.50
STATUTORY CLERK FEES   30.00
                                          TOTAL   482.50

The aforesaid purchaser having complied with the provisions of law applicable to such sales so as to be entitled to a certificate of purchase, on ██████████████ the Circuit Court of Cook County entered an order confirming the sale of the aforesaid property.

If the aforesaid property is not redeemed in the manner and within the time provided by law, said purchaser, his heirs or assigns shall be entitled, upon application and compliance with the Illinois Property Tax Code, to receive a deed to said property; provided, that unless the holder of this certificate shall take out said deed and file the same for record within one year after the time for redemption expires, the said certificate or deed, and the sale on which it is based, shall, from and after the expiration of such one year, be absolutely null.

WITNESS my hand and the ██████████████ in said
County this ███████ of ██████████████

countersigned:
███████████   ███████████

County Treasurer and Ex-Officio Collector   County Clerk of Cook County
        of Cook County

9

TAX DEED SALE

Some counties will purchase the taxes and go to deed on the properties if they were not purchased at the tax sale through a tax buyer. Each county will have either a tax deed sale or a scavenger sale.

The process for buying a tax deed directly from the county is not nearly as complicated as acquiring a tax certificate, and converting it into a tax deed. When buying a tax deed, the buyer receives a Quit Claim Deed directly from the county.

After receiving the deed from the county, the tax buyer must now file a suit for Quiet Title. The purpose for filing Quiet title is basically notifying anybody who might have a legal interest in the property to come forward. Quiet title is important because if a tax buyer attempts to sell the property in the future, title companies require proof that the title is clean. This is a quick and inexpensive process. It involves three steps:

1. The tax buyer's attorney must file a complaint for Quiet Title in the county where the property is located.
2. Summons and Notice by Publication must be put in a local paper. This is a legal way of notifying any parties who may have a legal interest in the subject property.
3. Affidavit of Service of Summons & Notice of Publication. Affidavit of Summons is additional proof that an effort was made to notify anyone who might have an interest in the property.

RE-OFFER TAX SALE

The Re-Offer tax sale occurs when the tax buyer does not pay the amount he bid for the certificate. This additional sale is offered after a tax deed or scavenger sale.

- ✓ Note: In some counties in Illinois, there may be civil penalties or a judgment levied if a tax buyer bids on a property and does not pay the bid amount. In other counties there are no consequences to the tax buyer for neglecting to pay.

OVER THE COUNTER PURCHASE

Another way of purchasing tax certificates is called an Over the Counter Purchase. If taxes were not sold at a tax sale, a tax buyer can now purchase them from the county clerk's office directly. This sale is not done through an auction.

QUESTIONS TO ASK PRIOR TO PARTICIPATING IN A TAX SALE

What is the goal of the investor?

The investor must know what his goals are when investing at a tax sale. Every investor has a different goal or objective.

Each investor has a different goal on what he wants to achieve. Some investors want to earn interest on the certificate purchased. In Illinois, tax certificates start at rates of 18% down to 0%. Others want to acquire the property by receiving a tax deed.

The investor must also take in to account which geographical areas that he wishes to invest in. He must consider which state, county, city, township, and streets of properties he has an interest in

How much money should the tax buyer invest at the tax sale?

Each investor must use his own judgment on the dollar amount he would be willing to tie up for the sale. Each investor's financial situation and goals are different.

The tax buyer must also consider the risk that they are willing to take on each parcel that they bid on. The more wisdom a tax buyer has going into the sale, the level of risk is considerably less.

Each tax buyer must take into account that unless the property is redeemed, the tax buyer will not receive any earnings on his investment for at least three years from the original purchase date of certificate. It will take approximately three years to receive a deed. The buyer looking to acquire real estate through the tax sale has to have patience. Properties that are redeemed by an owner will usually occur within one year of the tax sale.

The tax buyer must also consider all of the subsequent taxes that will be paid prior to receiving a tax deed.

Also, the legal fees for an attorney and applying for a tax deed must be taken into account when determining the cost of acquiring a tax deed.

What types of properties should I invest in?

The investor also must consider the type of property he wants to potentially acquire prior to bidding on the taxes. The tax buyer may bid on:

1. Single family homes
2. Multi- units
3. Vacant land
4. Farm land
5. Commercial property
6. Other property

How do I determine which geographical areas to invest in?

Research different cities throughout the state or states that you would be interested in

Find out if a city has a comprehensive plan. The comprehensive plan shows the detailed plan and goals of a particular city. The plan can be viewed by the public. It indicates where future placements of the following will be located geographically.

1. Infrastructure improvements
2. Retail developments
3. Residential developments
4. Industrial developments
5. Parks
6. Schools

Speak to city officials when possible. This will give the investor insight on what is developing in the city

Attend city council meetings whenever possible. The information discussed during these meetings address various present and future developments. The knowledge obtained at these meetings can give an investor a competitive advantage on where to invest geographically. It can also give an investor insight on what type of properties to invest in.

RESEARCHING FOR TAX DEED PROPERTIES

Intensive and thorough research is vital prior to investing in tax certificates or tax deeds. The more knowledge an investor has prior to bidding at the tax sale, the better chance of making a good investment. Researching for properties is tedious and time consuming.

Locate geographical area of interest. The tax buyer must first determine which areas he chooses to invest in. The investor should know which state, city, and neighborhood he desires prior to investing in tax certificates.

Study the Sidwell maps in the recorder of deeds at the county. This determines the exact size of the lot that the tax buyer may acquire. Be careful not to buy a lot that is not buildable, or does not have resale value. It is important to know the minimum size a lot must be in order to build a structure. Each municipality has different requirements.

Research the history of the property. It is important to study any legal activity that has occurred on the property at the recorder of deeds office. This will show any liens that are presently on the property. It is important to pay attention to the following type of liens.

1. IRS liens
2. Water liens
3. Demolition liens

4. Mortgages
5. Mechanics liens
6. Recorded rental liens
7. Lis pendens filed
8. Bankruptcy

✓ Note: Be aware that IRS liens, water liens, and demolition liens are not removed by a tax deed!

✓ Note: If the property owner is in bankruptcy court, then the property will end up a Sale and Error. A Sale and Error is a court order stating that the tax buyer's investment must be returned to him. In Illinois, the tax buyer will receive 10% interest on a Sale and Error. All of the other liens are extinguished by a tax deed.

Look through tax sale books in the county clerk's office. There are three books of importance. These three books show all of the tax payment history of a parcel of property.

1. **Judgment Books** - These books are also called the annual books and show all properties that were offered for sale during the annual sale.
2. **Scavenger Books** - These are the books from the sale that occurs every two years. Not all counties have a scavenger sale. Taxes sold at the scavenger sale have at least two years of delinquency.
3. **Warrant Books** - The warrant book has all real estate properties in it. This book is not as specific as the judgment or scavenger books. It gives a general outlook on any tax sale activity on a parcel of property.

✓ Note: The judgment and scavenger books are nearly identical.

These books show the following:

1. Tax certificate purchaser
2. Interest rate
3. Take notices (legal notification)

4. Extensions (legal notification)
5. Redemptions
6. Subsequent taxes purchased

The following illustration shows an example of an actual page from a Judgment book (annual book). The row appearing horizontally across the top explains what different activity that has occurred in each column.

Column #1 - Parcel I.D., owner's name, address of parcel sold for delinquent taxes
Column #2 - Volume number of parcel sold for delinquent taxes
Column #3 - Valuation by State Dept. (usually not important to tax buyer)
Column #4 - Special assessments owed on property
Column #5 - Interest on special assessment
Column #6 - Delinquent taxes owed
Column #7 - Interest due on late taxes (dated up until taxes are sold)
Column #8 - Total amount paid for tax certificate
Column #9 – Remarks {Indicates recorded Take Notices (Co. clk. notices), various filing fees recorded for acquiring deed}
Column # 10 - Subsequent taxes paid (Note: added into the redemption amount), extensions filed by attorney
Column # 11-Concludes the story on specific tax certificate. One of the following occurs

1. Property will be redeemed
2. Tax deed issued
3. Sale and Error will occur
4. Deed will not be issued. Column will remain blank.

Investors should drive by each parcel they are interested in bidding on. Also, the county assessor's website usually has pictures of each property in most counties. The tax buyer should use all resources available to make the tax buying process more efficient. After determining which properties qualify for the tax sale, it is time to move onto the tax sale.

TAX SALE PROCESS

The list of delinquent taxes on parcels of real estate can be located at the county department having the sale. The list is also publicized in local newspapers. The list is printed approximately one month prior to the sale.

Each county has their own rules and regulation manual. The manual lists the fees included in acquiring the tax certificate. Each county will have treasurer, clerk, and recording fees.

The manual states the security deposit money required for some tax sales, and the time frame the money must be deposited for security. This money deposited is for security only, and is not to be used for purchasing tax certificates. It is refunded approximately one month after the tax sale is complete.

Tax buyer in some counties will not allow the tax buyer to use post office box for his address. Each tax buyer must have a physical address.

The manual also addresses the consequences associated with not paying the amount accepted on the bid.

The location and time of the sale are also listed in the manual.

Pay close attention to when payments are to be paid on awarded bids. Typically they must be paid within 24 hours.

Seating arrangements are addressed in the manual. If the county has designated seating, it is important to attend the day designated seats are assigned.

✓ Note: It is best to have a bank account close to where payment is made. Fees must be paid via one of the following; cashier's check, money order, or cash.

An example of a detailed rules and regulation manual get be downloaded at **cookcountytreasurer. com**. Note: the manual will only be available approximately 1-2 months prior to the specific sale.

ATTENDING THE TAX SALE

Arrive early on the days that you are bidding at the sale.

Get a good seat. It is important the auctioneer can hear and see the bidder.

Be organized:

1. Organize parcel numbers of properties that buyer is bidding on.
2. Write down amount or percentage buyer wishes to bid.
3. Enlarge list of parcels that buyer is bidding on.

Be decisive during auction process. When finished bidding for day:

1. Receive bid sheet (this document states the amount owed by buyer)
2. Go to bank and get cashier check
3. Pay treasurer's office the amount owed
4. Go to the clerk's office and pay any additional fees

Do not lose receipts received from treasurer's and clerk's office. The receipts will be exchanged for the actual tax certificate within approximately 45 days.

The following illustration is an actual bid sheet, which is also referred to as a schedule of properties.

PROCEEDING TO TAX DEED

Prior to receiving the certificates it is vital to hire a tax deed attorney. This area of law is very specific and the tax buyer should avoid hiring a regular real estate attorney.

The legal process for going to deed is approximately a 2-3 year process. The rules for receiving an actual deed are specific, and an attorney cannot afford to make errors in this process. If an attorney makes an error in the process, the tax buyer could lose the right to receive the tax deed. The tax buyer could also lose the cash invested for the certificate.

The tax buyer exchanges the receipt received from the sale for the tax certificate. This is the beginning of the process of potentially receiving the tax deed. Upon receiving the certificate, any prior years owed on the taxes must also be paid, or the clerk's office will not give the buyer the tax certificate.

If the tax buyer chooses not to pay for any prior taxes owed on the parcel, the tax buyer cannot go to deed on the parcel. Instead, in Illinois, the buyer will still receive the certificate, but with a 5% stamp on it. The stamp indicates that the buyer will receive 5% if ever redeemed by an owner of the property in the future.

After receiving the tax certificate the attorney should file a **Take Notice**. The purpose of the Take Notice is to alert the owner that they can lose their property if taxes are not redeemed by a certain date. Time frames for an owner to redeem can vary from 6-36 months depending on the type of property. Vacant land sold for taxes can range anywhere from 6-24 months from day of purchase. Rental property can be redeemed within 24 months, and a homeowner must be given 30-36 months to redeem their property.

The owner still has the right to purchase subsequent taxes when the new tax bills are sent out. If the owner does not pay the new bills on time, the tax buyer can purchase any subsequent taxes on this parcel without going to the sale next tax sale. The subsequent taxes purchased by the owner can now be added on to the tax sale amount owed for redemption. In Illinois subsequent taxes receive interest at 12%/yr. After purchasing the subsequent taxes, proof of payment must be posted in the county clerk's office.

The tax buyer should go down to the clerk's office once a month to see if the taxes have been redeemed. If so, the buyer can turn the certificate in to the clerk, and receive the redemption amount owed to the buyer. Prior to the final redemption time, the buyer can now proceed to deed. The following fees must be paid in an effort to get the tax deed.

1. File a Petition for Deed
2. Serve Sheriff Notice
3. Law Bulletin Publication
4. Title Search

5. Court Reporter
6. Copy of Order
7. Issue Deed
8. Recording Deed

FINAL STEPS TO DEED

After the final redemption date has expired, the attorney for the buyer must now file a petition for deed.

The buyer and their attorney must appear before the judge to prove that legal process has been done by the petitioner/buyer. The attorney must show the following to the judge:

1. Proof that owner was notified through certified mail
2. Turn in original tax certificate to judge
3. Buyer must give legal description of property to judge.
4. The judge may have some questions, and have a few final requests. The judge will always ask the buyer to pay any present taxes due on the parcel.

If due diligence has been addressed properly, the judge will write a transcript advising the county to give a tax deed to buyer. The county will receive the transcript from the judge, and the county will then prepare a tax deed. The tax deed is typically received by tax buyer within 6- 8 weeks.

The Illinois Statute that addresses the legal process of tax deeds can be located online at **www.ilga.gov/legislation/ilcs/ilcs3.asp**. The state statute is (35 ILCS/Property Tax Code). Article 22 addresses Tax Deeds and Procedures. The specific areas that explain the legal process in its entirety are sections 22.5 to 22.90.

✓ Note: Record the deed immediately. All tax deeds must be recorded within one year after final redemption date or the deed is void

Name of Purchaser: _____ Reg. No.: _____

(STATE OF ILLINOIS) (SS.: COUNTY OF COOK)

SCHEDULE OF PROPERTIES

(Insert the Volume, Property Index Number and Date of Sale for each parcel upon which a bid was successfully made on behalf of undersigned purchaser by the undersigned bidder(s) Attach additional sheets if necessary.)

VOL.	PROPERTY INDEX NUMBER	DATE OF SALE
(1) _____	_____	_____
(2) _____	_____	_____
(3) _____	_____	_____
(4) _____	_____	_____
(5) _____	_____	_____
(6) _____	_____	_____
(7) _____	_____	_____
(8) _____	_____	_____
(9) _____	_____	_____
(10) _____	_____	_____
(11) _____	_____	_____
(12) _____	_____	_____
(13) _____	_____	_____
(14) _____	_____	_____
(15) _____	_____	_____
(16) _____	_____	_____
(17) _____	_____	_____
(18) _____	_____	_____
(19) _____	_____	_____
(20) _____	_____	_____

I (we) hereby affirm that I (we) successfully bid upon the above properties at the sale conducted by the County Treasurer of Cook County on the indicated dates, and I (we) request that the County Clerk of Cook County attach this schedule to my (our) application for Certificate of Purchase dated _____.

Signed under penalty of perjury as provided by law:

_____   _____
(Signature of Purchaser)   (Date)

_____   _____
(Signature of Bidder)   (Date)

24

TAKE NOTICE

County of ....Cook
Date premises sold.........................
Certificate No.:............................
Sold for General Taxes of 2002
Sold for Special Assessments of ....N/A
And Special Assessment No.: ....N/A
Warrant No.: ....N/A
Inst. No.: ....N/A

To: ████████   Volume: 430
████████
████████

THIS PROPERTY HAS BEEN SOLD FOR DELINQUENT TAXES

Property located at: The East side of ███████████████████████
███████

Legal Description or Permanent Index No.: ████████████

This notice is to advise you that the above property has been sold for delinquent taxes and that the redemption from the sale will expire on ████████████

This notice is also to advise you that a petition will be filed for a Tax Deed which will transfer title and the right to possession of this property if redemption is not made on or before ███████████

At the date of this notice the total amount which you must pay in order to redeem the above property is $451.25.

YOU ARE URGED TO REDEEM IMMEDIATELY TO PREVENT LOSS OF PROPERTY

Redemption can be made at any time on or before May 28, 2006 by applying to the County Clerk of Cook County, Illinois, at the County Building, ████████████████████████
███████████

The above amount is subject to increase at six month intervals from the date of sale. Check with the County Clerk as to the exact amount you owe before redeeming. Payment must be made by certified check, cashier's check, money order, or in cash.

FOR FURTHER INFORMATION CONTACT THE COUNTY CLERK

Dated:

Stephen Kon
Purchaser or Assignee

25

SALE AND ERROR

Under some circumstances the tax buyer can get his money back on tax certificates that should not have been sold by the county, or have liens that cannot be removed. The process is called a Sale and Error. The tax buyer can get a Sale and Error for one of the following issues.

1. Bankruptcy
2. Demolition lien
3. IRS lien
4. Storage tanks (fuel tanks)
5. Municipality owns property
6. County made error listing the taxes for sale

✓ **Note: The tax buyer will earn 10% interest on a Sale and Error certificate.**

The following illustration is an actual Sale and Error certificate issued by Cook County in the State of Illinois

OFFICE OF THE COUNTY TREASURER
COOK COUNTY, ILLINOIS
COUNTY BUILDING
118 N. CLARK STREET, ROOM 212
Chicago, Illinois 60602

COUNTY TREASURER ▬▬▬▬▬

RECEIPT
(FOR SURRENDERED CERTIFICATE OF PURCHASE)

BY SURRENDERING THE CERTIFICATE OF PURCHASE IDENTIFIED BELOW, THE TAX BUYER /ASSIGNEE, OR HIS ATTORNEY, REQUESTS THAT THE SALE IN ERROR REFUND ORDERED BY THE CIRCUIT COURT OF COOK COUNTY BE PREPARED.

DATE: ▬▬▬   COURT ORDER #: ▬▬▬

BUYER: Icon Investments   PHONE : ▬▬▬
ATTORNEY: Steve Kon
ADDRESS: P.O. BOX 241
CITY: Joliet   STATE: IL   ZIP: 60434

PIN #: ▬▬▬▬▬

VOLUME: ▬

CERTIFICATE#: ▬▬▬

TYPE OF SALE: SCAV

WARRANT #: N/A

SUBSEQUENT YR/YRS: NO

INTEREST: YES

RECEIVED BY: ▬▬▬

▬▬▬▬▬▬▬

27

TERMS AND DEFINITIONS

Annual Tax Sale - The public sale of a property that occurs every year by the county government for nonpayment of taxes.

Bid Sheet - The paper received by tax buyer at the end of each day of sales. Identifies the properties tax buyer paid taxes on.

Demolition Lien - A claim against property for removal of structure; usually lien is not removed by tax deed.

Extension - A legal document that allows the owner of property additional time to redeem.

IRS Lien - claim against property by Internal Revenue Service for unpaid income taxes

Lien - a right given by law to certain creditors to have their debts paid out of the property of a defaulting debtor, usually by means of a court sale.

Lis Pendens - A notice that literally means a lawsuit pending that is usually recorded but sometimes filed so as to give constructive notice to warn all persons that the title or right to the possession of the real property is in litigation

Mortgage - A conditional transfer or pledge of real estate as security for the payment of a debt. Also, the document creating a mortgage lien.

Quitclaim Deed - A conveyance by which the grantor transfers whatever interest he or she has in the real estate, without warranties or obligations.

Redemption Period - The time the owner of the real estate is allowed to recover the rights to the property without losing ownership because of involuntary alienation.

Scavenger Deed - A deed conveyed to tax buyer through a public sale of land for non-payment of property taxes; taxes must be delinquent two or more years to be auctioned.

Sidwell Maps - Land maps provided by county offices (recorder of deeds) that indicate where a specific property is located in a geographical area within that county.

Scavenger Sale - The public sale of a property by the county government for the nonpayment of taxes that are two or more years delinquent.

Subsequent Taxes - Property taxes that are due to the county dated after the initial date of tax purchase; subsequent taxes must be paid prior to obtaining tax deed.

Tax Certificate - A certificate purchased at a tax sale which transfers the lien, but not the title to the tax buyer. If taxes are not redeemed by the redemption date, the property may potentially be transferred to tax buyer by involuntary alienation.

Take Notice - Legal notice filed by tax purchaser that notifies real estate owner that property taxes were sold for a specific property. Indicates on notice that property will be lost if not redeemed by a certain date.

Tax Deed - A deed conveyed by involuntary alienation to a tax buyer through public sale of land for delinquent taxes.

Tax Deed Sale - Public sale of real estate by a county that sells the specific property. Title is conveyed by a quitclaim deed.

Warrant Book - Legal property tax book produced by each county that indicates general property tax information.

Printed in the United States
by Baker & Taylor Publisher Services